P9-CNI-017

IRISH PROVERBS

ILLUSTRATED BY *Karen Bailey*

CHRONICLE BOOKS
SAN FRANCISCO

First published in 1986 by
The Appletree Press Ltd
19-21 Alfred Street
Belfast BT2 8DL
Tel. +44 1232 243074
Fax +44 1232 246756

Irish Proverbs

First published in the United States in 1986
by Chronicle Books, 85 Second Street,
San Francisco, California 94105

Web Site: www.chronbooks.com

Distributed in Canada by
Raincoast Books
8680 Cambie Street
Vancouver, B.C. V6P 6M9

ISBN 0-8118-1532-3

9 8 7 6 5 4 3 2 1

what's good for the goose
is good for the gander.

The older the fiddle
the sweeter the tune

It's no use boiling
your cabbage twice

8

There's no need to
fear the wind
if your haystacks are
tied down

Do not mistake
a goat's beard for
a fine stallion's tail

Drink is the curse of the land.
It makes you fight with
your neighbour. It makes
you shoot at your landlord—
and it makes you miss him.

If you lie down with dogs
you'll rise with fleas

A wild goose never
reared a tame gosling

A boy's best friend is his
mother & there's no
spancel stronger than
her apron string

There never was an
OLD SLIPPER
but there was an
OLD STOCKING
to match it

Firelight will not let you
read fine stories but it's
warm & you won't see the
dust on the floor.

As the old cock crows
the young cock learns

Humour, to a man,
is like a feather pillow.
It is filled with what is
easy to get but gives
great comfort

Many an Irish property
was increased by the lace
of a daughter's petticoat

The best way to keep loyalty
in a man's heart is to keep
money in his purse

A narrow neck keeps the
bottle from being emptied
in one swig

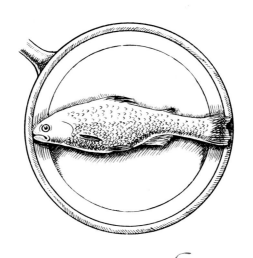

A trout in the pot
is better than
a salmon in the sea

If the knitter is weary
the baby
will have no new bonnet

It's for her own good
that the cat purrs

Even a tin knocker
will shine on a dirty door

An old broom knows
the dirty corners best

One beetle
recognizes another

To the raven
her own chick is white

when the sky falls
we'll all catch larks

Any man can lose
his hat in a fairy-wind

If you have one pair of
good soles it's better than
two pairs of good uppers

It's no use carrying an
UMBRELLA
if your shoes are leaking

It's difficult to choose
between two blind goats

A silent mouth is
sweet to hear

It's as hard to see a
woman crying as it is to
see a barefooted duck

He'd offer you an egg if
you promised not to
break the shell

It's a bad hen
that won't scratch herself

No matter how often a
pitcher goes to the water
it is broken in the end

There was never a
scabby sheep in a flock
that didnt like to have
a comrade

A nod is as good as a wink
to a blind horse

The fox never found a
better messenger than
himself

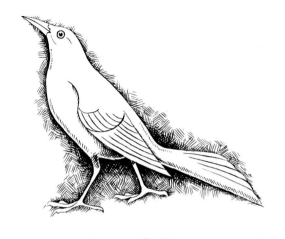

There'll be
WHITE·BLACKBIRDS
before an unwilling woman
ties the knot

Show the fatted calf but
not the thing that
fattened him

A buckle is a great
addition to an old shoe

In winter the milk
goes to the cow's horns

Men are like bagpipes:
no sound comes from them
till they're full

Snuff at a wake is fine
if there's nobody sneezing
over the snuff box

You must crack the nuts
before
you can eat the kernel

Every patient is a doctor
after his cure

Neither give cherries to
pigs nor advice to a fool

Soft words butter no
parsnips but they won't
harden the heart of the
cabbage either.

You'll never plough a field
by turning it over in
your mind

There are
FINER · FISH
in the sea
than have ever been
CAUGHT

A Tyrone woman will
never buy a rabbit
without a head
for fear it's a cat

*A windy day is
not the day for thatching*

The old pipe gives
the sweetest smoke

Marriages are all happy
It's having breakfast
together that causes all
the trouble

A scholar's ink
lasts longer than
a martyr's blood

Take gifts with a sigh,
most men give to be paid

DECEMBER
25

A turkey never voted
for an early Christmas

what butter & whiskey
will not cure
there's no cure for

The Irish forgive their
great men when they are
safely buried

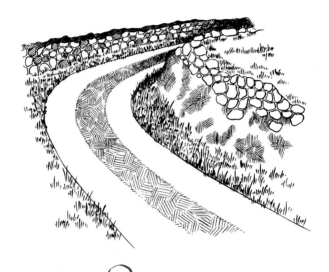

The longest road out
is the shortest road home